D0574395

MATTER

Please visit our web site at: **www.garethstevens.com**
For a free color catalog describing Gareth Stevens Publishing's list of high-quality books and multimedia programs, call 1-800-542-2595 (USA) or 1-800-387-3178 (Canada). Gareth Stevens Publishing's fax: (414) 332-3567.

Library of Congress Cataloging-in-Publication Data

Matter.—North American ed.
    p. cm. — (Discovery Channel school science: Physical science)
    Originally published: Transform. Bethesda, Md: Discovery Enterprises, 2000.
    Summary: Explains how everything on Earth can be grouped into four states of matter and how matter can change from one state to another by applying heat or pressure. Includes related activities.
    ISBN 0-8368-3361-9 (lib. bdg.)
    1. Matter—Properties—Juvenile literature. [1. Matter—Properties.] I. Title. II. Series.
QC173.36.T73   2003
530—dc21
                                   2002030532

This edition first published in 2003 by
Gareth Stevens Publishing
A World Almanac Education Group Company
330 West Olive Street, Suite 100
Milwaukee, WI 53212 USA

This U.S. edition © 2003 by Gareth Stevens, Inc. First published in 2000 as *Transform: The States of Matter Files* by Discovery Enterprises, LLC, Bethesda, Maryland. © 2000 by Discovery Communications, Inc.

Further resources for students and educators available at www.discoveryschool.com

Designed by Bill SMITH STUDIO
Project Editors: Justine Ciovacco, Lelia Mander, Sharon Yates, Anna Prokos
Designers: Nick Stone, Sonia Gauba, Bill Wilson, Darren D'Agostino, Joe Bartos, Dmitri Kushnirsky
Photo Editors: Jennifer Friel, Scott Haag
Art Buyers: Paula Radding, Marianne Tozzo
Gareth Stevens Editor: Betsy Rasmussen
Gareth Stevens Art Director: Tammy Gruenewald

Printed in the United States of America

1 2 3 4 5 6 7 8 9 07 06 05 04 03

Writers: Jackie Ball, Stephen Currie, Robin Doak, Dan Franck, Chana Stiefel, Denise Vega, Diane Webber, Christina Wilsdon, Sharon Yates

Editor: Sharon Yates

Photographs: Cover, © Corel; p. 2, candle, © PhotoDisc; p. 2, flames, © PhotoDisc; p. 3, glassblower, Andy Sacks/Tony Stone Images; p. 3, world, MapArt; p. 5, candle flame, © PhotoDisc; p. 8, Fire, © PhotoDisc; p. 8, Robert Boyle, Archive Photos; p. 9, pollen, © PhotoDisc; p. 10 girl, © PhotoDisc; p. 10, astronaut's meal, NASA; p. 11, cake,© PhotoDisc; p. 12, hands with beakers, © PhotoDisc; p. 12, Las Vegas, © PhotoDisc; p. 12, flame, © PhotoDisc; p. 13, ocean, © PhotoDisc; p. 14, Joseph Priestley, © Bettmann/CORBIS; p.14, mouse, © PhotoDisc; p. 16, *Endurance*, Underwood & Underwood/CORBIS; p. 22, Archimedes, Bettmann/CORBIS; p. 23, hand computer, Ron

Leighton; p. 24, glass melting, © Andy Sacks/Tony Stone; p. 25, aluminum, © PhotoDisc; p. 28, Dr. Ramon Lopez, courtesy of Dr. Lopez; p. 31, brain, © PhotoDisc; all other photographs, © Corel.

Illustration: p. 20, Lee MacLeod.

Acknowledgments: pp. 14-15, "The Story of 'Good Air'" excerpted from EXPERIMENTS AND OBSERVATIONS ON DIFFERENT KINDS OF AIR by Joseph Priestley, Second Edition, 1776; p. 16, background information about the Endurance from THE ENDURANCE by Caroline Alexander, Alfred A. Knopf, NY, 1999; p. 25, background about aluminum, Ohio Department of Natural Resources; p. 27, Richard Posner; p. 30, quotations from CHARLIE AND THE CHOCOLATE FACTORY by Roald Dahl, Alfred A. Knopf, NY, 1964.

CONTENTS

Everything Matters

Everything on Earth—you, this book, your classroom, the world—is made of matter. Matter can be a solid, a liquid, or a gas. (Plasma is also matter, but it is rarely found on Earth.) You can't escape matter, but you can transform it: change it from one state to another, using heat or pressure.

In *MATTER,* Discovery Channel takes you on a tour of the different states of matter. Ice, water, oxygen, gold, glass—each has a fascinating story to tell. Even your own body has three states of matter—solid, liquid, and gas.

Matter describes what happens when matter changes from state to state. Sometimes the results are delicious, such as a cake after it's been baked. Sometimes the results are dramatic—think of lava during and after a volcanic explosion.

After reading this book, you may never look at yourself or the world around you again in quite the same way. We guarantee: you'll be transformed!

States of Matter 4
At-a-Glance A burning candle is a marvel of matter: it's a solid, liquid, and gas—all three at the same time. It also has a fourth state of matter: plasma.

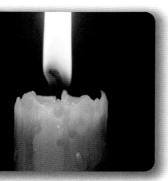

Shape Shifter 6
Q & A Oxygen is invisible, but it sure has a lively lifestyle. Check it out. It's a gas!

All That Matter 8
Timeline Solids, liquids, and gases seemed like very different matters to early scientists.

What a State I'm In! 10
Picture This Can you take the heat? Discover what happens to some of our favorite foods when they take the heat.

Matter of Fact 12
Almanac Some matter leaps over the liquid state and goes directly from solid to gas, never enjoying the pleasures of being poured. Find out how this happens and lots of other amazing facts about matter.

The Story of "Good Air" 14
Eyewitness Account Two mice help Joseph Priestley discover the good air (oxygen) in the air all around us. Priestley's curiosity also leads him to make the first-ever "fizzy water"—what we now call carbonated water.

Chill Out! 16
Scrapbook If you think ice can only keep things cold, don't skip over this page. You'll also be introduced to ice calves and find out why the tip of the iceberg is a clue to bigger things.

Solid as a . . . liquid?
See page 24

Earthly Matters 18
Map When matter changes from state to state, we're not talking Oregon to Oklahoma. We mean volcanoes, geysers, rain forests, and other dramatic places around the world.

You, Matter 20
Virtual Voyage Just like the world around you, the world inside you is made up of solids, liquids, and gases. Take the tour and see what kind of stuff you're made of.

The Legend of the Gold Crown and the Bathtub . . 22
Scientist's Notebook Did the goldsmith cheat the king? The king's friend, the great math whiz Archimedes, figures it out when he takes a bath. Both the story and solution are more than 2,000 years old!

Secrets of Matter 24
Amazing but True When is a glass a liquid? Is it true a solid can bend and stretch? And be gooey, too? Here are some of matter's best stories for you.

The Case of the Stained-Glass Windows 26
Solve-It-Yourself Mystery Join Detective Vapori and use your knowledge of matter to decide if the stained-glass windows are fake or the real thing.

Plasma—Why It Matters 28
Heroes There's not much plasma here on Earth, but the rest of the universe is full of it. Physicist Ramon Lopez tells us how it may change our lives

Laughing Matters 30
Fun & Fantastic Take a quiz, sample the fizz, and jiggle the gelatin. Also, find out why your homemade ice cubes come out cloudy.

Final Project
What's the Matter? 32
Your World, Your Turn When it comes to matter, the world is in balance—solids, liquids, and gases. But what if Earth lost its balance? And how can you help keep "matters" under control?

Albert Einstein once said that science is just an extension of everyday thinking. His point was that if you were to think deeply about everyday things, you would come to some sort of scientific understanding of the world around you.

This book is called *MATTER*. It presents to you some of our knowledge of states of matter. In it, you will learn about solids, liquids, gases, and about a fourth state of matter called plasma. These might seem like way-out science topics, but in fact, some of the most common experiences of our everyday lives—rain, snow, the air we breathe—have a lot to do with the states of matter that make up our world.

Look closely at the burning candle on this page. It is something so common that we take it for granted. Not much there at first glance. But in the 1800s Michael Faraday, one of the greatest scientists of all time, used a single candle to teach an entire course on chemistry and physics. Each day he would come before class and light the candle, and each day he would explain something else about why it worked the way it did. A candle, far from being a simple occurrence, is a marvelous thing and gives us the chance to see in action all of the states of matter.

SOLID STATE—A solid is the state of matter in which the matter retains its shape. A candle is made from a kind of solid wax called paraffin. Paraffin has a low melting point. Some cheap candles can even melt on a hot day, but mostly a candle is wax that stays solid at a normal room temperature.

The tip of the wick burns because it is in the hotter part of the flame. The bottom of the wick is in the cooler part of the flame, so it doesn't burn.

PLASMA STATE—At the tip of the flame, the temperature is so hot that part of the rising gas is transformed into a fourth state of matter called plasma. As part of that reaction, light and heat are released.

GASEOUS STATE—A gas is a state of matter in which the matter fills all the available space. The heat from the flame causes some parts of the paraffin to transform from a liquid to a gas. The gas then reacts with heat and the oxygen in the air (another gas), and the whole reaction gives off light and heat. The gases rise up towards the tip of the candle.

LIQUID STATE—A liquid is a state of matter in which the matter takes the shape of any surrounding container. If there is no container, the liquid will flow. In this case, heat from the flame transforms the paraffin into its liquid state. We call this "melting." The liquid paraffin pools at the top of the candle. It also runs down the candle. There, where the heat is less, the running liquid cools and the paraffin transforms back into the solid state. Back at the top of the candle, some of the liquid climbs upward along the fabric of the wick.

Shape-Shifter

Q: You're oxygen. Nice to see you. Well, we can't really see you, but you know what I mean. Thanks for being here for this week's broadcast of Matter Matters.

A: Nice to be here. But then again, I'm everywhere. Oxygen makes up about a fifth of Earth's atmosphere.

Q: Very impressive. For someone who gets around so much, it's surprising no one has ever seen you.

A: Not really. Gases are invisible—transparent and colorless. Not all of us are odorless, of course.

Q: So we've noticed. Do you ever wish you had a definite color or shape, like a solid or a liquid?

A: Not at all. Being shapeless is what makes being a gas such a gas! I never know where I'll be next . . . what shape I'll assume. I could be in a little kid's birthday party balloons . . . pumped into a spare tire. . . blown into a life raft. Imagine how dull—how FLAT— the world would be without gases. A hunk of something solid can't take different shapes like a gas.

Q: No, but a liquid can. Ladle soup into a mug and the soup is mug-shaped. Pour it into a plastic bag, you've got bag-shaped soup.

A: True, true. But liquids have their limits. Two cups of hot chocolate won't fit into one cup. Half of it will slop over the top. You can't stuff a brick into a salt shaker . . . or a St. Bernard into a suit. That's because liquids and solids have definite volume.

Q: And gases don't have a definite volume?

A: Correct. You can keep pushing and pumping more and more of us into the same space. We expand or contract to fit—at least up to a point. Put too much of me in a balloon and it will burst. And we fill that available space evenly. We don't sink to the bottom in a heap like a liquid.

Q: So what's your secret?

A: One word: energy. Gases are loaded with energy. The tiny particles we're made of have so much energy they can fly around in every direction, spread out and stay away from each other. Solid particles don't even have enough energy to crawl from one place to another. They huddle together in a tired mass. Think of a hunk of cheese. A slab of wood. A pile of rock. Talk about a boring life.

Q: How about liquids? How's their energy level?

A: Liquids are a little livelier. Their particles have enough energy to move over and around each other, but not enough to stay apart. When you pour something liquid, the particles stream and flow over each other. But eventually they gather back into a pool or puddle.

Q: Is there any way liquids and solids can get any more energy? Some kind of high-energy diet?

A: The best way is to turn up the heat. Heat is a wake-up call for couch particles. When they feel the heat, the particles start hopping. You can see it happen every time you heat a pan of water. The surface gets active. Tiny gas bubbles form. If the water boils, big bubbles break the surface and gas with water vapors in it rises—steam.

Q: Wait a minute. Gas! You're talking about changing matter from one state to another.

A: Good thinking! Increasing or decreasing heat can change matter to a different state. If you melted an ice cube, you'd be adding heat—and changing a solid into a liquid. And increasing the activity of the particles. Almost any solid will lose its shape if it's heated enough. And if most matter is heated to 9000° F (4982° C) or more, it becomes the fourth state of matter—plasma. That's where the particles are wild with energy.

Q: Well, you've certainly been a breath of fresh air on our show.

A: Uh-Uh. Air isn't just oxygen. Good thing, too—pure oxygen burns. That's why I'm often found in combination with other elements such as hydrogen to make water. But whatever—it's been a pleasure being here. I'll be seeing you—but don't bother looking for me.

Activity

MELTDOWN What is the fastest an ice cube can melt? What is the slowest? Try this. Take four ice cubes (as nearly identical in size as you can find), and place each one in a glass or shallow bowl. Place each container in a different temperature situation, such as a window sill, the refrigerator (not the freezer), and a tabletop. Hold one about six inches above a lit candle. Invent your own situations. Take the temperature of each situation and note how long each ice cube takes to melt completely. Now make a line graph of time of melting versus temperature. When all the data are recorded, extend the line graph and see if you can determine the fastest and slowest melting times.

All That Matter

530-450 BC	Around 450–150 BC	1620	1646	1660

The Greek philosopher Anaximenes states that air is the "primary substance" of the universe. Air thins and becomes hot, he claims, turning into fire and forming the Sun and stars. He says that air shrinks, becomes cold, and turns into wind, clouds, rain, rock, and soil. If he had used the word matter, he would have been right.

The Greek philosopher Heraclitus proposes that everything in the universe is in a constant state of change. He believes that fire is the primary substance in the universe.

Empedocles, a Greek philosopher and doctor, teaches that fire, air, earth, and water are the universe's basic substances. These four substances change into other substances as they mix together and separate.

Other Greek philosophers base their ideas on those of Empedocles. Plato suggests Earth is made of tiny bits of material shaped like cubes. The philosopher Democritus states that everything in the world is made of tiny particles of matter called "atoms" that move about and can't be broken down into anything smaller. Changes happen, he says, when atoms collide.

Flemish chemist Johann Baptista van Helmont measures the "air" produced by burning wood—namely, carbon dioxide. This marks the first time a scientist studies the gases produced by a chemical reaction. Van Helmont calls the shapeless substance chaos. He spells it "g-a-s," because that's what chaos sounds like in his language. The name sticks.

French scientist and mathematician Blaise Pascal discovers that the force of pressure applied to one area of a liquid or gas is spread throughout it equally. This happens because liquids and gases are fluid, taking the shape of whatever container they're in. Pressing on one spot puts pressure on all parts. Pascal's discovery is later called "Pascal's Law" and leads to the study of hydraulics—how things can use fluid and pressure to work. A car's brake system is one example.

Irish chemist Robert Boyle discovers that squeezing a gas into a smaller area increases the pressure of the gas. He also discovers the mathematical relationship between the amount of pressure applied to the gas and the amount of space taken up by the gas. This formula is still called Boyle's Law. It's used today, for example, in scuba-diving tanks. A scuba diver's tank can hold enough oxygen, under pressure, for the diver to breathe comfortably underwater.

Robert Boyle

In ancient times, people considered solids, liquids, and gases to be very different things. They didn't know that matter is composed of small particles, which we call atoms and molecules. Today, we know that solids, liquids, and gases are all "states of matter"—phases of the same substances. Hydrogen, for example, is a gas on Earth, but under high pressure on Jupiter, it's a liquid. Iron is a solid on Earth's surface but near the planet's core, it's a liquid.

Scientists also study a fourth state of matter: plasma, a sort of electrified gas that exists in lightning, neon lights, semiconductors, and the Sun's solar wind. It may form most of the matter in the stars and the universe.

How did we reach today's conclusions about matter? It took a lot of thought and a lot of years.

1738

Swiss mathematician Daniel Bernoulli shows how a gas exerts pressure if it is made up of many tiny particles (atoms and molecules) that move quickly and strike a container's walls. He also explains how the speed of a fluid (gas or liquid) relates to pressure: the faster a fluid flows, the lower the pressure it exerts. This is called Bernoulli's Law and explains how air flow works to lift an airplane.

1756-1787

English chemist Joseph Black proves gases can react with solids and liquids. He also shows that ordinary air contains carbon dioxide.

French physicist Jacques Charles invents the hydrogen balloon and flies one mile into the air. He shows how a gas expands as it warms and contracts as it cools—even though the pressure applied to the gas stays the same. The gas, however, exerts more pressure when it is heated. That's how Charles gets liftoff. Charles also figures out the mathematical relationship between the rate of expansion and the temperature. This discovery is called Charles's Law.

1827

Looking through a microscope at a liquid, English botanist Robert Brown sees tiny bits of pollen jiggling inside it. He assumes the pollen itself is moving. Later experiments show the motion speeds up when the temperature is raised. This molecular activity is later called Brownian motion.

1905

The German-American physicist Albert Einstein explains Brownian motion. He figures out how molecules in motion can make tiny particles, such as pollen, move about. The molecules push the pollen in different directions. This is the first evidence that molecules and atoms actually exist.

1929

American chemist Irving Langmuir coins the term *plasma* to describe the behavior of electrons and charged particles in a gas given off in an experiment. The term is new, but the discovery isn't. Fifty years earlier, the English scientist Sir William Crookes noticed this "ionized gas" and claimed that it could possibly be a fourth state of matter.

Magnification of Pollen

Activity

WHAT'S IN A NAME?
You've read how philosophers and scientists of the past used the terms chaos, plasma, liquid, solid, and gas. Get out your dictionary and find out how these terms are used by others. Write a sentence for each one.

PICTURE THIS

What a State

Like all other forms of everyday matter, food comes in three basic states: liquid, solid, and gas. To change a food from one state to another—say, from solid to liquid, or liquid to gas—you need to turn up or down the heat. Here are some examples of foods in flux!

MELTDOWN

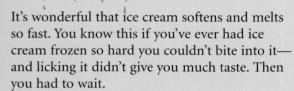

It's wonderful that ice cream softens and melts so fast. You know this if you've ever had ice cream frozen so hard you couldn't bite into it—and licking it didn't give you much taste. Then you had to wait.

Ice cream freezes at about 29°F (-1.7°C), slightly below the temperature at which pure water freezes. The water in the ice cream is frozen solid; its particles are moving relatively slowly. When you remove ice cream from a freezer, you're warming it up. The air's heat makes the water particles start to move more rapidly, melting the ice cream into a drippy (and delicious) liquid mixture of water and cream.

Spacey meal

Usually, solids turn into liquids and liquids change to gases—in that order. (Think of solid ice melting into liquid water and then evaporating into thin air.) Can a solid change directly into a gas without changing to a liquid first? Just ask an astronaut or a backpacker! They often eat freeze-dried foods because they're easy to pack and prepare, they don't spoil, and most important, they weigh less than regular food.

Here's how freeze-dried foods, in this case, peas, are made: First, the peas are frozen solid. Then they're placed in a vacuum (an airless container, not the machine that cleans your carpets) to speed up the process. Ice particles on the peas' surface absorb heat from the container and break free, vaporizing (turning to gas) instead of water. This process, called sublimation, removes about 90 percent of the water from the peas and leaves a concentrated solid. To eat the peas, you just add water. What freeze-dried foods can you find in your supermarket?

I'm In!

Steam machine

If you want to see water in three states, you don't have to travel to New York, California, and Florida. With an adult, melt solid ice cubes in a pot on the stove until they turn to liquid water. Carefully boil the water until steam rises.

Here's the tricky part. Most people (adults and kids) think steam is a gas. But, if you can see it, it isn't a gas. When water reaches very high temperatures, it vaporizes, or turns into an invisible gas called vapor. You can't see water vapor, but it's there—at the gap between the boiling water and steam.

So what's steam? A liquid mist! When the vapor rises, it cools and condenses, forming tiny liquid water droplets of steam.

Bake me a cake

It always seems like magic. The thick, mushy batter goes into the oven and out pops a cake. But what's really going on in there? First, the oven's heat makes the water in the cake batter evaporate (turn to vapor) at temperatures just above 212° F (100° C). (Here's a well-kept secret: Even though your oven is set to 350° F (175° C), the temperature inside the cake never rises above 212° F (100° C). The evaporating water keeps the batter cooler than the temperature inside the oven.) The proteins in the eggs interact and form an interlocking network that lets the cake batter solidify. Bet you never thought chemistry could taste so good!

Activity

HOT CAKES Imagine you're the head baker at The Chocolate Unlimited Bakery. You're supposed to deliver a special birthday cake today to the Matter Middle School. Your oven, though, is acting up and won't get hotter than 200° F (100° C). You need it to be at 350° F (175° C). But you figure this is just 12° F less than the temperature the inside of the cake will get anyway. You decide to go ahead and bake the cake longer at the lower temperature until it is done. You don't want to disappoint the kids. Will your plan be successful? Write out your reasons and draw a picture of the finished cake. Check out the explanation on page 32.

Matter of Fact

All matter is made up of tiny particles called atoms. Matter is usually seen in three common states: solid, liquid, and gas. A fourth state, plasma, is less a part of our everyday lives. All matter can undergo physical or chemical changes and change from one state to another. Just think about water, a liquid. Ice and water vapor are just different states of the same matter!

Check out some of the properties of the three basic forms of matter below.

Solids

- Have a definite size and shape.
- Feel hard to the touch.
- May be changed to liquids when heated. This process is called melting.
- May be changed directly to gases. This process is called sublimation.
- Can be elastic. Some solids, like a rubber band, can spring back into shape after being compressed.
- Can be molded and have their shapes changed.

Liquids

- Have a definite size, but not a shape. Feel wet and can be poured.
- Take the shape of the container they are in.
- May be changed to solids by freezing. May be changed to gases by heating. This process is called vaporization.
- Are not elastic.
- Spread out evenly within their container.

Gases

- Have neither a definite size nor shape.
- May not be visible and cannot be touched or felt.
- Gases have weight.
- May be changed to liquids by cooling or compressing.
- Spread out evenly within their container.

Plasma: The Fourth State of Matter

- Scientists have identified a fourth state of matter, called plasma. This type of plasma is not the same as blood plasma. Instead, it is matter in which the atoms in certain super-hot gases have taken on a high-energy electrical charge. Plasmas are completely different from any other form of matter, including other gases.
- Nearly 99 percent of matter in our universe is in the plasma state. Stars, the Sun, comet tails, the Northern Lights, and lightning are all plasmas. On Earth, however, plasmas are not common.
- So where can you find plasma on our planet? Check out a neon sign. When neon gas is charged with electricity, it changes to the plasma state. That is how it gives off light. Fluorescent lights are another example of plasma in action.

Hot and Cold

The freezing point of a liquid is the temperature at which it changes to a solid. A liquid's melting point—the temperature at which it changes from a solid to a liquid—is the same as its freezing point. Ice melts into water at 32°F (0°C). Water freezes at 32°F (0°C). A liquid's boiling point is the temperature at which it changes to a gas. Here are the freezing, melting, and boiling points of some common liquids.

LIQUID	FREEZING AND MELTING POINT	BOILING POINT
Water (at sea level)	32°F (0°C)	212°F (100°C)
Ethanol (alcohol)	-170°F (-112°C)	173°F (78°C)
Auto antifreeze	-26°F (-32°C)	219°F (104°C)
Window cleaner	32°F (0°C)	212°F (100°C)
Mercury	-38°F (-39°C)	674°F (357°C)

Skip the Liquids!

Some matter can change directly from solid to gas or from gas to solid, completely skipping the liquid state. This process is known as sublimation. Sublimation can occur when a substance is rapidly heated or cooled.

Solid carbon dioxide, also known as dry ice, is a substance that sublimes. Dry ice changes directly from a frozen solid to a vaporous gas when it is heated.

An even more common example of the sublimation process is snow. Snow starts off as air that has been saturated, or filled, with water vapor. When the saturated air is quickly cooled to below freezing, it becomes a snowflake—a solid!

Water: An Amazing Liquid

Water is the most common liquid on Earth

- Water is the only naturally occurring substance that can be found on Earth in all three states: ice, water, and vapor.

- More than 70 percent of Earth is covered with water, yet only 1 percent is actually usable fresh water!

- Each person in America uses between 80 and 100 gallons of water each day.

- Unlike most matter, water is less dense in its solid state than its liquid state. That's why ice floats in water!

- Water takes up a thousand times more space as a vapor than as a liquid.

- More substances can be dissolved in water than in any other liquid. This is why water is called the universal solvent.

The Air We Breathe

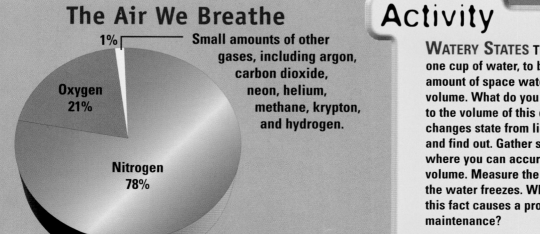

1% Small amounts of other gases, including argon, carbon dioxide, neon, helium, methane, krypton, and hydrogen.

Oxygen 21%

Nitrogen 78%

Activity

WATERY STATES Think about water—one cup of water, to be precise. The amount of space water takes up is its volume. What do you suppose will happen to the volume of this cup of water as it changes state from liquid to solid? Try it and find out. Gather several containers where you can accurately measure the volume. Measure the volume again after the water freezes. Why do you suppose this fact causes a problem in highway maintenance?

The Story of "Good Air"

Joseph Priestley befriended American inventor and politician Benjamin Franklin in 1765, while Franklin was working in London. Sharing an interest in electricity, the two became friends. At Franklin's urging, Priestley studied and wrote about electricity. Later, while living in Leeds, Priestley observed strange air rising from the brewery next to his house. He soon began to experiment with "airs"—today, we call them "gases."

In his book, *Experiments and Observations on Different Kinds of Air,* Joseph Priestley writes of separating "good" air from "common" air. Below are excerpts from Priestley's book, describing how, on August 1, 1774, he discovered "good" air—oxygen—and later went on to confirm his conclusions with two cooperative mice.

". . . a candle burned in this air with a remarkably vigorous flame, very much like that enlarged flame with which a candle burns in nitrous air, exposed to iron or liver of sulphur; but as I [had] nothing like this remarkable appearance from any kind of air besides this particular modification of nitrous air, and I knew no nitrous acid was used in the preparation of mercurius calcinatus, I was utterly at a loss how to account for it."

Mercurius calcinatus was mercuric oxide, an orange-red or orange-yellow powder used mainly as a pigment in paints. In Priestley's time it was also found in ointments for skin problems. When burned at a high temperature, it emits oxygen, which Priestley captured and stored. Oxygen is needed for fire to burn, so it makes sense that pure oxygen would create what Priestly called "a remarkably vigorous flame."

"I conclude that it was between four and five times as good as common air. It will be seen that I have since procured air better than this, even between five and six times as good as the best common air that I have ever met with."

Priestley did not know that he had just identified oxygen. As Priestley watched the flame burn brightly, he wondered: What would happen to a living creature in this "good" air?

"On the 8th of this month [March 1775] I procured a mouse, and put it into a glass vessel, containing two ounce-measures of the air from mercurius calcinatus. Had it been common air, a full-grown mouse, as this was, would have lived in it about a quarter of an hour. In this air, however, my mouse lived a full half hour; and though it was taken out seemingly dead, it appeared to have been only exceedingly chilled; for, upon being held to the fire, it presently revived, and appeared not to have received any harm from the experiment.

... For my farther satisfaction I procured another mouse, and putting it into less than two ounce-measures of air extracted from mercurius calcinatus and air from red precipitate ... it lived three quarters of an hour. But not having had the precaution to set the vessel in a warm place, I suspect that the mouse died of cold. However, as it had lived three times as long as it could probably have lived in the same quantity of common air, and I did not expect much accuracy from this kind of test, I did not think it necessary to make any more experiments with mice."

And thus, with the help of two brave mice, Priestley confirmed that he had isolated this "good" air from the common air we all breathe. But after he recorded his results, his own curiosity got the better of him. Priestley decided he had to try the air himself, and breathed it in using a glass-syphon. He described the sensation this way:

"... the feeling of it to my lungs was not sensibly different from that of common air; but I fancied that my breast felt peculiarly light and easy for some time afterwards. ..."

Renowned French chemist Antoine-Laurent Lavoisier would later name this air "oxygen." Though Lavoisier, Swedish chemist and pharmacist Carl Wilhelm Scheele, and Priestley all "discovered" oxygen, Priestley was the only one who documented and published his results immediately, thus getting official credit.

Bouncing Bubbles

Before Joseph Priestley "discovered" oxygen, he had made another discovery—one that many people enjoy today. Priestley was curious about the gas that was produced in the brewery next door to his house. It drifted to the ground, indicating that it was heavier than normal air. When he made this "heavy gas" in his home lab and dissolved it in water, Priestley found that the mixture had a "very pleasant and tangy taste." Priestley called it "fixed water." What Priestley had done was mix the gas carbon dioxide in the water. This made the water fizzy. In 1773, Priestley was awarded a medal from the Royal Society for his discovery of "fixed water." Today, we find Priestley's fixed water in the form of bubbles in carbonated beverages, otherwise known as soda water and soda pop.

Priestley the Prophet

When Joseph Priestley tried oxygen himself, he wrote: "Who can tell but that, in time, this pure air may become a fashionable article in luxury. Hitherto only two mice and myself have had the privilege of breathing it. ..." His prediction has come true as people today flock to oxygen bars, paying good money to breathe in pure oxygen. Former competitive swimmer Lisa Charron opened the first oxygen bar in North American in 1996. Based in Toronto, she called it the O_2 Spa Bar. Customers in need of a soothing rest visit frequently to breathe in their favorite flavored oxygen.

Activity

THE BREATHING TREE **Plants absorb carbon dioxide and release oxygen. Watch a tree or other plant breathe with this activity. You'll need a plastic bag, a twist tie, and a tree or other plant with leaves you can reach easily. (Remember, needles on evergreen trees are leaves, too.) Find leaves that get lots of sun. Cover them with a plastic bag and seal it with a twist tie. Go back the next day and examine the bag. What do you see? What's your explanation?**

CHILL OUT!

What's Cool about Ice and Snow

Brrr! Journey south to Antarctica, the land of ice and snow, and you'll be plunged into temperatures as low as -76°F (-60°C). You don't have to travel that far to freeze your fingers, however. Just visit the freezer part of your refrigerator—or "icebox," as this piece of machinery was once called. It may be as cold as 0°F (-18°C) in there!

Ice is the solid form of water, which freezes at 32°F (0°C). It is an unusual solid because it is less dense than water—that is, its molecules are less tightly packed. That's why water expands when it freezes—and why ice floats in your glass of water.

Ice may be freezing cold, but because it contains lots of air, it is also a good insulator. This means ice can actually keep some things warm! A pond's surface may freeze in winter, but beneath the ice, fish may be swimming in water that's as warm as 39°F (4°C). That's not very warm—but it's positively tropical compared to the chilly weather above the ice!

Likewise, mice and other small mammals scurry about in tunnels underneath snow, where it's warmer. Snow is made of ice crystals loosely packed together. Some birds, such as the chunky ptarmigans of the Arctic, even fly headfirst into snowbanks to roost!

A Tale of Endurance

In August 1914, British explorer Sir Ernest Henry Shackleton and his crew of twenty-seven set out in a ship called Endurance for Antarctica. Their goal was to be first to cross the ice-covered continent. By January 1915, ice in the Weddell Sea had closed around the ship, freezing it into place for the next ten months. Eventually, the ice crushed the ship, and the crew had to abandon it in October. It sank on November 21, 1915. The crew dragged three lifeboats and supplies onto a ice floe, where they were stranded until April 1916—nearly six months. When the ice began to break up, the men piled into the open lifeboats and rowed to Elephant Island, avoiding being crushed by the huge ice blocks in the sea.

It took them seven days to reach the uninhabited island with its towering glaciers and icy mountains. They were suffering from frostbite, thirst, and other maladies. They had no shelter and no hope of anyone even knowing where they were—but they were on solid ground for the first time in 497 days.

Shackleton knew he had to go for help. After a few days, he took five men and set off in one of the lifeboats. Their destination was South Georgia Island, 800 miles (1,287 km) away. Despite the navigational hazards and snow and hurricane-force winds, they made land sixteen days later. They were wet, dehydrated, and frostbitten. But their journey was still not over. The whaling station was on the other side of the ice-covered mountains. Shackleton and two others made the trek. They reached the station three days later. Bad weather, ice, and other delays prevented Shackleton from returning to Elephant Island and rescuing his crew until August 30, 1916. This was four months after he had left in the lifeboat, and two years since they had left England. Not a single life had been lost. These sailors did more than endure in perhaps the harshest environment on Earth; they triumphed over it.

Cold Calves

Some glaciers are so huge, they cover a mountaintop. They're called ice caps. When ice caps cover bigger areas, like the continent of Antarctica, they're called ice sheets. Icebergs are formed when a big chunk of ice breaks off from one of these ice masses and plows into the sea. The process is called calving, and it's very noisy. Loud roars and groans rumble from the ice when it calves. One iceberg that was calved in 1996 was bigger than the state of Rhode Island!

In a Fog

Have you ever seen clouds of vapor billow across the stage at a concert? The clouds are often puffs of the gas carbon dioxide, given off by chunks of dry ice. This is an example of sublimation.

Under Pressure

An ice skater twirls on the ice. As she spins, she seems to be raised slightly from the ice, as if she were floating on air. In actuality, she is floating—

on a thin layer of water created by her skates. The sharp blades of her skates press into the ice beneath her weight. This pressure causes the ice to melt. The skates' blades slide along on the water. After the skater passes and the pressure is removed, the water refreezes.

The Tip of the Iceberg

Icebergs are very dangerous obstacles to ships. In 1912, the *Titanic* struck an iceberg on its maiden voyage across the Atlantic. The ship sank and about 1,500 people drowned. Icebergs are like frozen, floating mountains. They can be a few miles long and as high as a 30-story building.

But it's what a ship's pilot can't see that's the most hazardous: the part of the iceberg under the water. Like all ice, icebergs float, but only their tops stick out of the water. The bulk of the ice lurks beneath the waves—and that bulk can be nine times bigger than the part you see above the water!

Today, satellites monitor the movements of icebergs, and ships are warned to steer away from them.

Activity

COLD STORAGE Freeze a half cup of water and a half cup of melted ice cream in separate plastic containers. Record how long it takes each to freeze. Then record how long it takes for them to melt at room temperature. Graph your findings. Can you think of a possible explanation for the results?

Earthly Matters

Whether it's solid, liquid, or gas, matter in its different states creates some unusual places and events—some spectacular, some deadly—around the world.

Yellowstone National Park
Geysers are fountains of steam and hot water that shoot high into the air from an underground tunnel.

Kilauea, Hawaii
When a volcano explodes, it blasts out tons of red-hot lava, ash, and gases—such as smelly sulfur dioxide and poisonous carbon monoxide. Lava is melted rock from deep inside the earth. As it cools, it hardens back into rock.

NORTH AMERICA

Amazon Rain Forest, Brazil
It's hot, humid, and—you guessed it—rainy in a rain forest. A minimum of 70 inches (1.8 meters) of rain falls each year. When rain forests are burned, the thick vegetation releases carbon dioxide gas.

SOUTH AMERICA

Earth's Core The very center of Earth is an inner core made of solid iron and nickel. It's surrounded by a core of liquid iron nickel. Yes, liquid metal. It's so hot down there that the metal liquifies. There's more pressure on the inner core, so it stays solid.

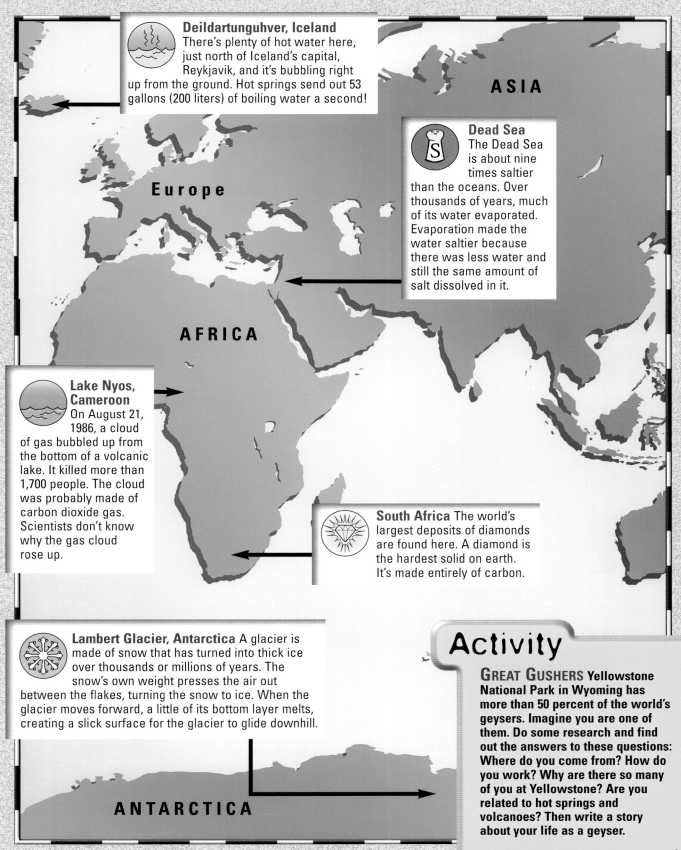

Deildartunguhver, Iceland
There's plenty of hot water here, just north of Iceland's capital, Reykjavik, and it's bubbling right up from the ground. Hot springs send out 53 gallons (200 liters) of boiling water a second!

ASIA

Dead Sea
The Dead Sea is about nine times saltier than the oceans. Over thousands of years, much of its water evaporated. Evaporation made the water saltier because there was less water and still the same amount of salt dissolved in it.

Europe

AFRICA

Lake Nyos, Cameroon
On August 21, 1986, a cloud of gas bubbled up from the bottom of a volcanic lake. It killed more than 1,700 people. The cloud was probably made of carbon dioxide gas. Scientists don't know why the gas cloud rose up.

South Africa The world's largest deposits of diamonds are found here. A diamond is the hardest solid on earth. It's made entirely of carbon.

Lambert Glacier, Antarctica A glacier is made of snow that has turned into thick ice over thousands or millions of years. The snow's own weight presses the air out between the flakes, turning the snow to ice. When the glacier moves forward, a little of its bottom layer melts, creating a slick surface for the glacier to glide downhill.

ANTARCTICA

Activity

GREAT GUSHERS Yellowstone National Park in Wyoming has more than 50 percent of the world's geysers. Imagine you are one of them. Do some research and find out the answers to these questions: Where do you come from? How do you work? Why are there so many of you at Yellowstone? Are you related to hot springs and volcanoes? Then write a story about your life as a geyser.

You, Matter

Y es, you do.
Matter, that is.
And yes, you are. Matter.
And not just one kind of matter. You
may look like a solid hunk of human, but
your body includes matter in the liquid and gas
states, too. If you could travel through a human
body, where would you see the different states of
matter? You've come to the right place to find out—the Virtual Voyage
Launching Pad. All you do is compress yourself into a mini-self the size
of a human cell. Call yourself Micro-me.

Speaking of cells, these basic building blocks of the human body are made mostly of a watery liquid called cytoplasm. The cell's soft outer covering is solid and is called a membrane. Other solid inner parts of the cell are the nucleus, nucleolus, and mitochondria. Gas? Cells take in oxygen and get rid of carbon dioxide. In a way, every human cell could be called a micro-you.

Strap on those tiny wings and let's fly! Just follow an air current right up a nostril. Watch out! Those nose hairs may look flimsy, but they're solid. They have to trap dust particles. Now you're passing over the moist mucous membrane that warms the air before it travels into the lung. Now you're headed down the trachea toward the lungs. You follow the bronchial tubes through smaller and smaller branches until you reach the hollow end of the breathing system. You squeeze through the cell walls and immediately ditch the wings and kick into a microscopic set of swim fins. You're in the capillaries—the tiniest branches of the bloodstream—swimming with the red blood cells.

The capillaries in the lungs are a busy place. This is where oxygen gas enters the liquid bloodstream and carbon dioxide, the waste gas of cells, comes out. Notice the thin film of liquid on the cell walls? It's water—the water needed to dissolve the carbon dioxide for the trip out. On most days, we exhale about four cups of water.

Swimming in the bloodstream is slow since blood is three times thicker than water. But since blood makes up almost half of the liquid in the body, it's the best way to see the sights. Riding in the tide of blood, you will be making almost countless stops—namely, to every cell in the body. Red blood cells are really hardworking membranes that carry gas—oxygen— as part of their hemoglobin molecules.

You swim into the small intestine, where liquids called gastric juices have been breaking solid food into small enough pieces to join the bloodstream. The dissolved solid nutrients are carried to the liver, the body's warehouse. You travel to the kidneys, where both solids and liquids are turned into liquid waste—urine.

You visit lots of other organs and soon the trip starts getting tiring. Like other red blood cells, you're running out of gas—oxygen. You're also running out of sugar, or glucose, since that's the solid food the blood cells have been dropping off. And the bloodstream is picking up liquid and gas waste: water and carbon dioxide. A trip back to the lungs is necessary so the body can get rid of the stuff. Quick— kick off your fins and fasten your wings. The body is getting ready to exhale—and out you fly again!

Activity

STATE OF SURPRISE You've made a quick tour around the body and found matter existing in more states than you might have thought. Now take a virtual vacation to another place, looking for matter that may exist in surprising states. Use the Internet and books for your research. Write a letter home about your "trip." Try exploring the ocean (commonly thought of as liquid) for solids and gases, or a mountain (commonly thought of as solid) for liquids and gases. Or find a place in the world where matter

The Legend of
The Gold Crown

The Wise One. The Master. The Great Geometer. These were a few of the nicknames given to the Greek mathematician Archimedes, a man who forgot to stop for meals when he was hard at work on a mathematical problem. He often gave advice to the ruler of Sicily, King Hiero II, who was his friend.

One day, Hiero II asked Archimedes to help him solve a problem. Hiero II had hired a goldsmith and had given him a block of gold weighing a specified amount to use to make a gold crown. When the crown was finished, Hiero II weighed it. It weighed the same as the gold block the king had given the goldsmith. Yet Hiero II had a sneaking feeling that the goldsmith had cheated him and had used silver as well as gold in the crown and kept the unused gold for himself. How could this be proved without spoiling the crown?

Archimedes mulled over the problem. It was still on his mind one day as he stepped into his bathtub. Water splashed over the edge of the tub as Archimedes settled into it. As the water dripped, a realization popped into the great mathematician's mind: the water he splashed out of the tub when he got in was equal to the volume taken up by his body.

At that moment, Archimedes knew he had the key to Hiero II's dilemma. More water splashed on the floor as he leaped out of the tub and, without even stopping to grab a towel, dashed out of the house. He ran down the street, shouting "Eureka!" which means "I have found it" in Greek. No doubt the citizens of Syracuse wondered what the great mathematician had lost as he bolted through the town. His mind, perhaps?

and the Bathtub

Luckily for us, Archimedes was quite sane, even though he was forgetful about ordinary things, such as towels and clothes. But what did the water in the bathtub have to do with Hiero II's crown and its metal content?

Well, Archimedes knew that a piece of gold weighs more than a piece of silver the same size. According to legend, Archimedes weighed the king's crown. Then he got a piece of pure gold that weighed the same amount as the crown. He placed the gold into a bowl of water, measured how much it made the water rise, and took the gold out.

Next, he put the crown into the water and saw that it made the water rise higher than the piece of gold had. Why? Because this crown was larger than one made of pure gold. The goldsmith had to make the crown larger when he substituted silver for some of the gold so that the crown would weigh the same as a pure gold crown. But the silver-gold crown took up more space in the bowl and made the water rise higher.

Because Archimedes took a bath, the dishonest goldsmith was now in hot water!

2,000 Years Later

Modern historians note that there are some things wrong with the Archimedes story. Nobody knows for sure whether Archimedes ran through Syracuse naked, for one thing. More important, the difference in the amount of water displaced by a pure gold crown and a silver gold crown is so small that it couldn't have been measured using the tools that existed in Archimedes' time. Also, water would cling to objects as they were taken out, which would distort the results. But even if the story is wrong in its details, Archimedes' principle has remained true for the past 2,000 years!

Activity

FLOAT IT! Scientists today call Archimedes' discovery the Archimedes Principle. It states that an immersed object is "pushed up" or buoyed up by a force equal to the mass of liquid it displaces. What does this mean? Liquids push up against the bottom of objects. This is buoyant force. Objects float when the buoyant force of the liquid is greater than the weight of the object. A big and heavy object floats when the force of the water pushing up against it is greater than its weight. Two objects can have the same mass, yet one might sink while the other one will float. This happens when one has the mass spread out more, taking up more space for the water to push against.

To test this idea of buoyant force, get a piece of clay about the size of a golf ball. Work it into different shapes, testing each shape to see if it sinks or floats. What are you holding constant by using the same ball of clay? What are you changing?

Secrets of Matter

A Glass Act

Quick! Answer this question: Is glass a solid or a liquid? That's too easy, you say. Of course it's a solid. Liquids flow. You can pour tea, but you can't pour a mirror. Besides, liquids fill the shape of their container. Water in a bowl immediately takes on the round shape of the bowl. Water in a box takes on the square shape of the box. But a piece of glass inside a bag won't change its shape, not even if you wait a week or a year.

Well, for a very long time, scientists categorized glass as a liquid (a "supercooled" liquid). To find out why, let's take a look at how glass is made. The raw materials of glass are solids: ordinary sand mixed with powders such as lime or soda ash. These materials are melted together in a furnace at temperatures approaching 2,372° F (1300° C). To make the mixture into glass, the liquid is cooled. The cooler it gets, the harder it becomes. By the time the temperature reaches the levels found outside on a typical day, it is hard enough to be viewed as a solid.

But some liquids flow slowly. Think about ketchup, shampoo, or maple syrup; they're all pretty slow compared to water. But they're still liquids. Historically, scientists believed glass was similar. Its flow was just painfully slow—so slow you couldn't see it move.

The proof was thought to be found in the windows of very old buildings—ones built a couple of centuries ago or more. The glass in these windows is thicker at the bottom than at the top. It was believed that, over time, glass had oozed to the bottom, molecule by molecule. It isn't as strange as it sounds. The arrangement of glass molecules is similar to those of a liquid; they are not in a fixed arrangement like molecules of a solid, so it is possible that they might flow.

But in 1998, a study claimed that the thick-bottomed glass in old windows was not the result of glass flowing. Rather, the panes of glass had been of an uneven thickness when made, and were installed with the thicker edge at the bottom. The study had calculated the amount of time it would have taken for old glass in windows to flow—longer than the existence of the universe!

So, is glass a solid or a liquid? The debate goes on. But one thing is true: Glass is an amazing substance. But don't try pouring any on your pancakes tomorrow morning.

It's a Stretch

HERE'S A RIDDLE: What solid can you bounce, stretch, and bend? Answer: rubber. You can't do this with most solids—just try stretching a nickel or bending a diamond. You can even erase pencil marks with rubber. Imagine doing that with a slice of bread!

When supplies of rubber were low during World War II, the American government asked chemists to create a new kind of rubber. James Wright took up the challenge and experimented with combining boric acid and silicone oil. The result was smooth and easy to mold, just like natural rubber. It stretched and bounced, too, like the regular stuff. But Wright's new rubber had some special qualities. It stretched further than rubber. It bounced higher. It could keep its form, even in extreme temperatures. It could pick up near-perfect ink impressions if held against a line of writing. And it could even pick up loose cat hairs from the couch.

Unfortunately, Wright's new rubber was not suitable for making rubber tires or industrial equipment, so he gave up working on the project. But visitors to his lab enjoyed playing with the slippery stuff. Bouncing it, stretching it, lifting images of comic strips from the daily papers, and oozing it, liquid-like, between their fingers.

The story might have ended there, except that a toy dealer named Paul Hodgson got hold of a sample of Wright's artificial rubber. Buying $147 worth of Wright's invention, he packaged one-ounce chunks inside plastic eggs and sold them. By 1949, the goo-filled eggs were Hodgson's bestseller. Still popular today, they're known as—you guessed it—"Silly Putty™."

YOU CAN

Aluminum is one of Earth's most plentiful metals, a solid. Much of it is used for packaging products, such as soda, frozen-foods, and foil. We use a lot of aluminum in cans for beverages. In 1996, the United States produced a staggering ninety-nine billion cans. Thank goodness we recycle!

Recycling involves collecting and melting the cans, changing their state from solid to liquid. New cans are formed from the liquid aluminum. One million pounds of aluminum cans melt in four hours. It takes only sixty days for a can to be collected, melted, and reformed, and back up on the shelf in your grocery store, sparkling new.

Companies can make twenty recycled cans with the same amount of energy it takes to make one can from scratch. Changing the states of cans is much better than letting them pile up in our waste disposal sites for the next two hundred years.

Activity

A MATTER OF IMAGINATION Imagine that you can create a brand-new product by simply changing its state of matter or its characteristics. Here are two ideas to get you started: paper that evaporates and chocolate you can lick without its getting smaller or losing its flavor. Give your product a name and write an advertisement describing its benefits.

The Case of the

Stained-Glass

Detective Valerie Vapori had been on the case of the missing Elixir Windows since the beginning. Three of the five stained-glass works of art, which once hung in the Elixir Castle, were stolen from the Matterville Museum years ago. She had dutifully followed every lead in the case, but the mystery remained unsolved. So when Sammy Slick called her office with information about the three hundred-year-old treasures, Detective Vapori was all ears.

"You've got to come down to my sister's lawn furniture factory, Slick Aluminum. I think you'll be very interested in what I've just found here," Mr. Slick said.

Detective Vapori rushed over to meet Sammy, his sister, Sylvia, and their cousin, Carey Cagey, the carpenter. They led her to the back of a huge, cluttered, dusty room, and there Sammy pulled back a burlap sack with a flourish. "Voila!" he exclaimed. "I've found the Elixir Windows. The thieves must have stashed them here. Isn't this wonderful?"

"It's a wonder, all right," Detective Vapori said, guardedly.

"The Matterville Museum offered a handsome reward for the return of the windows, I recall," Sylvia Slick said. "When do you think Sammy can collect it?"

"Just as soon as we do some tests on these windows," Detective Vapori replied. "We want to make sure they're the real thing, after all."

A SOLID SEARCH

Detective Vapori took the newly discovered windows back to the Matterville Museum where she could compare them to the other two Elixir Windows, which she knew were authentic.

The first things she looked at were the outer wooden frames that held the windows. Matterville Museum's master craftsman, Woody Wellner, made the frames after the museum inherited the precious windows from the Elixir family. She called Woody in to examine the frames on the windows found by Sammy Slick.

"Those are my frames all right," Woody said. "I can tell because the wood is the same, aged oak. And the shellac is the same."

"How can you be so sure? Couldn't a good carpenter easily copy the wood and the shellac?" Detective Vapori asked.

"Yes, they certainly could," Woody answered, "but I also signed and numbered the back of each frame on the lower, right corner. And these frames definitely have my signature. The numbers

Windows

are also correct. I can confidently say these are the original frames I made for the Elixir Windows."

THICK OR THIN?

Next, Detective Vapori looked at the colored glass itself. Very old glass panes are often thicker at the bottom than at the top. The two windows hanging in the Matterville Museum had glass panes that were one to three centimeters thicker at the bottom.

Of the three windows found at Slick Aluminum, two showed no thickening in the glass. The panes of one window, however, were about one centimeter thicker at the bottom than at the top.

"Very interesting," Detective Vapori remarked.

WHAT A GAS

Now, it was time for Detective Vapori's final test: the flame test on the metal structure between the pieces of stained glass. Chemists and physicists use flame tests to identify certain metallic elements. Different metals emit different colors of light when exposed to the flame of a Bunsen burner. The flame, which needs oxygen—a gas found in the air—to burn, provides energy to excite the electrons in the metal's atoms. (When the electrons are excited in this way, the metal is,

very briefly, in the plasma state, which is the fourth state of matter.) The color we see during the flame test is a result of the electrons returning to lower energy levels.

Detective Vapori wanted to find out what kind of metal was in each of the windows. When she tested the two windows from the Matterville Museum, the color emitted was blue-green. Two of the windows from Slick Aluminum burned blue-white. The last window (the one whose glass showed signs of flow) burned blue.

THINK TANK

What do you think Detective Vapori concluded about the authenticity of the three Elixir Windows at Slick Aluminum? What do you think her next move should be? Give reasons for your answers. Then check the solution on page 32.

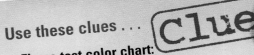

Use these clues . . . Clues

▶ Flame test color chart:
Copper—blue-green
Calcium—brick-red
Lead—blue
Sodium—golden-yellow
Aluminum—blue-white

▶ Stained-glass windows are traditionally made using lead, copper, or cement as the structure between the colored panes of glass.

Plasma—
Why It Matters

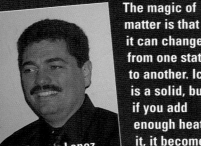
Dr. Ramon Lopez

The magic of matter is that it can change from one state to another. Ice is a solid, but if you add enough heat to it, it becomes a liquid. Add more heat, and it becomes vapor, a gas. But what happens if we take steam and subject it to extremely high temperatures? The answer is surprising. The water atoms begin to come apart. Add more heat, and the electrons start to separate from the atoms. This separation allows the steam to conduct electricity. It also causes it to be sensitive to magnetic forces. The result is a constantly flaring, erupting, and seething substance. Doesn't sound like any steam you've ever seen? You're right. It's something different—an entirely new state of matter called plasma. Scientists call plasma the fourth state of matter.

Plasmas are rare compared with the more ordinary liquids, solids, and gases that we see every day. "We don't interact much directly with plasmas here on Earth," comments Dr. Ramon Lopez, a pioneer in the study of plasmas. True, there are only a few plasmas around. Neon and fluorescent lights are both plasmas. Some industrial processes, too, make use of plasmas. Etching tiny circuit routes onto computer microchips is one example. Still, it doesn't seem as if plasmas would affect daily life very much. Or do they? Television relies on plasma. Satellites that beam programs across the globe couldn't do their job if we didn't know how plasma affected them. The screens of laptop computers also use plasma.

But if we look beyond Earth, the percentage of plasma changes dramatically. "Most of the universe is in the plasma state," says Lopez. Some people think plasma accounts for 99 percent of all matter. This figure includes the spaces between stars, the solar wind produced by

the Sun, and even the inside of stars.

Studying plasma can help us understand more about our own planet and the forces that create its movements. Physicists are hard at work trying to use plasmas to help build alternate sources of energy; someday we may heat our homes with plasma-based nuclear fusion, the same process that powers the stars themselves. In short, Lopez sums up, research into plasmas will impact us more and more as time goes on.

Lopez's path to studying plasmas began early. "I became interested in atoms when I was in the sixth grade," Lopez remembers, "and decided then

When you look at the beautiful colors of the Northern Lights, you are seeing plasma.

Plasma is used to create neon signs.

that I wanted to be a physicist." Why physics? "It was the most fundamental science," he explains. "Physicists try to understand the basic workings of the universe." His interest in atoms was sparked partly by doing experiments at home. Lopez's parents bought him a Radio Shack circuitry kit, a chemistry set, and a telescope, each of which let him learn science by doing science.

Lopez's scientific studies were also spurred by events in the world around him. "These were the years of the *Apollo* missions and the first landing on the Moon," Lopez points out. The sense of wonder and curiosity about the solar system and deep space was important to Lopez; his curiosity has only grown stronger. "In the end," he says, "it was my early fascination with space that determined my career."

Lopez went on to earn a bachelor's degree in physics from the University of Illinois and a doctorate in space physics from Rice University in Houston. He worked for several research institutes and universities before joining the University of Texas at El Paso in 1999, where he is a professor and chairman of the physics department.

Lopez has spent much of his time explaining plasma and physics to kids, hoping they will become as enthusiastic as he is. Toward this goal, he has helped develop a traveling museum exhibit called "Electric Space: The Plasma Universe" and another called "Electric Space: Bolts, Volts, and Jolts from the Sun."

Still, Lopez's first passion is space. He continues to design and run experiments that will shed even more light on the mysteries of plasma and the environment of space surrounding Earth. The results of his research may be purely theoretical—or they may change the world as surely as have the microchip and the satellite.

Activity

NORTHERN LIGHTS You can see plasma at work in neon and fluorescent lights. Plasma is also at work in the aurora borealis (Northern Lights) and the aurora australis (Southern Lights) that light up the skies with brilliant colors. One person described the Northern Lights as "dancing fairy lights." They are caused by plasma in the solar wind. Many cultures have stories or legends about how the Northern Lights came to be. Find other pictures of these spectacular light displays in books and on the Internet. Create your own story or legend describing the origins or purpose of the Northern Lights, and illustrate it with paints or markers.

Laughing Matters

JIGGLY GELATIN

What is the state of gelatin? When mixed with water, it flows slowly and takes the shape of a cup or bowl. But when it cools, it keeps its form like a solid. When you add hot water (a liquid) to gelatin powder (a solid), the proteins in the mix dissolve and form a strong 3-D network. When you chill the mixture, the protein network holds on to the water to form that jiggly gel.

Candyland

Check out these luscious liquids, silly solids, and burpy gases that appear in *Charlie and the Chocolate Factory* by Roald Dahl:

"Every drop of that river is hot melted chocolate of the finest quality . . . There's enough chocolate in there to fill every bathtub in the entire country!"

"Hot ice cream warms you up to no end in freezing weather. I also make hot ice cubes for putting in hot drinks. Hot ice cubes make hot drinks hotter."

"FIZZY LIFTING DRINKS . . . 'They fill you with bubbles, and the bubbles are full of a special kind of gas, and this gas is so terrifically lifting that it lifts you right off the ground like a balloon . . . '"

"Humor me ..."

Q: Why did the chemist like working with hydrogen so much?

A: Because it was a gas.

Crystal Clear?

Ever wonder why the ice in your freezer is always cloudy? It never looks like glass or the perfect ice cubes used in commercials for soda. The reason is because there is always a little dissolved air in tap water. The temperature and pressure of air, once it gets into the ice trays, keeps it as a gas, and so it forms bubbles in the ice. These make your ice cubes cloudy. Commercial ice machines (like those you find in hotels) make crystal-clear ice by making sure the concentration of air in the water never gets too high as it's frozen.

20 QUESTIONS

Try this new variation of an old game. Think of a solid, a liquid, or a gas. It can be something obvious (such as milk) or outrageous (such as marshmallows). Tell your friends which state of matter you have in mind. Then have them guess the object you're thinking of by asking no more than 20 "yes or no" questions. The friend who guesses your object wins. Then it's his or her turn to choose a solid, liquid, or gas. If no one guesses the right answer, you win.

Brain Teasers

1 Atoms in a liquid are farther apart than in a gas. True or False?

2 What force pulls liquids towards the ground?

3 *Burp!* What beverage is a mixture of a liquid and a gas that you sometimes pour over a solid?

(See Answers on page 32.)

Now that you've read this book, you know that everything in the world, including you, is made of matter. You know that there are four states of matter and you also know that matter can change its state if enough heat or pressure is applied or taken away.

The balance of the states of matter on Earth creates an environment that allows life to flourish. But suppose this balance of liquids, solids, and gases were to change? It could happen. Warmer temperatures could be the cause. The year 1998 was the warmest in the last 1,200 years! In the future, Earth's climate will be warmer still—unless we take preventative measures. The ratio of gases in the air may change because of the greenhouse gases, which contribute to global warming. There may be fewer trees and more solid wastes. Warmer temperatures could cause the polar ice caps to begin to melt. What would these changes in the balance of matter do to life on Earth?

For your Final Project, divide a group of friends or classmates into three sections: solids, liquids, and gases. Have each section find out the answers to the questions below about their particular state of matter. Listen to each section's report on how a change of its state of matter would affect Earth. Then, all together, brainstorm what people can realistically do to keep the states of matter—and life on Earth—in balance.

Solids At what temperature would the polar ice caps begin to melt? What effect would melting polar ice caps have on the land mass? On people?

Rain forests and other forests are being cut down. How do trees affect gases and liquids? (Hint: Think of weather and gases in the air. Don't forget about the role of roots.)

Why is the build-up of solid waste a problem?

Liquids How much would the polar ice caps have to melt before large-scale flooding occurred?

Will melting ice affect temperature? Will less ice mean even warmer temperatures and thus more flooding?

What will happen to the oceans? How will this affect the land and Earth's climate?

Can the extra water from the ice caps be used? To drink? For power?

Gases Find out how much global temperatures have increased in the last century. Is there a difference in the rate of increase over the decades? Graph your findings.

Based on current annual temperature increases for Earth, predict what the temperature might be 25 years from now. How will this affect human life, life in lakes and oceans, crops, and disease?

What effect will fewer trees have on our air?

Research the sources of the greenhouse gases: carbon dioxide, ozone, methane, nitrous oxide. How do they affect our climate? What will their impact be if we don't control the release of these gases into our atmosphere? Read a little about the atmosphere and temperature of Venus and compare with Earth's.

ANSWERS

Solve-It-Yourself Mystery, pages 26–27:

All three Slick Aluminum windows are copies of the Elixir Windows. One of them is a very good copy—old glass and a lead structure were used. But the real Elixir Windows are made of copper, and the glass is much older. The other two were cheap fakes made with new glass and aluminum.

Detective Vapori's next move was to search the Slick Aluminum factory where she found the three, authentic Elixir Windows. Then she arrested Sammy Slick, Sylvia Slick, and Carey Cagey. They confessed to taking Woody Wellner's oak frames off the original windows and putting them on the Slick's counterfeits.

Hot Cakes, page 11:
Baking would take so long that the outer layer would dry out and even burn, while the inner layers may not get hot enough to rearrange the proteins. Result: Overdone outside, underdone inside. A flop! Better get that oven fixed quick!

Answers to Brain Teasers, page 31:
1) False: atoms in liquids are closer together than atoms in gas.
2) Gravity pulls liquid—and all substances—towards the ground. It also flattens the surface of liquid.
3) Soda pop. It has water (liquid) and bubbles of carbon dioxide (gas) to make it fizz. You sometimes pour it over ice cubes (solids).